Right: *Stegosaurus.*
Previous pages: A museum's
reconstruction of two *Tyrannosaurus*
prowling around a kill.

COVER: *Tyrannosaurus* **seizes the**
duckbilled dinosaur *Corythosaurus.* **Top**
row of box: The skull of a sauropod;
Brachiosaurus **browse the treetops. Centre**
of box: Fossil leaf. Bottom of box:
a fossil in the making; *Styracosaurus,* **a**
dinosaur from the Cretaceous period.

-THE WONDER BOOK OF-

DINOSAURS

WARD LOCK

Contents

Editorial

Author Ron Taylor

Designer Keith Groom

Editor Angela Royston

First published in Great Britain 1981 by Ward Lock Limited, 47 Marylebone Lane, London W1M 6AX, a Pentos Company.

© Grisewood and Dempsey Limited 1981

Designed and produced by Grisewood and Dempsey Limited, Elsley Court, 20—22 Great Titchfield Street, London W1.
All rights reserved.
Printed in Portugal by Gris Impressores S.A.R.L.

British Library Cataloguing in Publication Data
Taylor, Ron
Dinosaurs — (Wonder Book)
1. Dinosaurs — Juvenile literature
I. Title
567.9'1   QE862.D5

ISBN 0 7063 6132 6

Dinosaurs

You have probably seen at least one film about prehistoric times, featuring gigantic, scaly monsters. Roaring hideously, these huge reptiles advance on the hero and heroine with gaping, many-fanged jaws, giving the audience a pleasant thrill of terror. Such an idea of the extinct reptiles called dinosaurs is not exactly exaggerated or untrue, because many dinosaurs were indeed huge and terrifying beasts. But dinosaurs died out millions of years before human beings appeared on Earth. No one has ever seen a living dinosaur. We know they existed because of fossils which help us to reconstruct them, as shown at the end of the book.

Like many other land animals, dinosaurs descended from water animals, the fishes. Our story of the dinosaurs begins on the next page with these fishy ancestors. From the fishes came the amphibians which could breathe air and survive on land but which still largely depended on the water for life. From the amphibians came the reptiles, the first really successful land animals. Most spectacular of all the ancient reptiles were the dinosaurs, rulers of the Earth for 160 million years.

Triceratops

Dinosaur

From Fins to Feet

(1)

(2)

A

C

B

D

(3)

A

C

B

D

The direct ancestors of dinosaurs were fish which lived more than 350 million years ago. They were lobefins, so called because they had a fleshy lobe in each fin and could use their fins as legs. Lobefins were good swimmers and had primitive lungs which enabled them to survive periods of drought.

Gradually, over thousands of years, the legs and tails of lobefins grew longer and stronger and they evolved into the earliest amphibians—ancient relatives of the frogs, toads and newts of today. These were the first large land animals.

Both the lobefins and the early amphibians left many fossil bones in the rocks. (Fossils are described on page 28.) The diagram on the left shows that the fin bones

◀ **The first land animals descended from fishes. Fossil bones of the fins of these fishes, (1) and (2), resemble those of the limbs of the early amphibians (3).**

Ancestors

of early lobefins (1) and (2) were similar to the leg and foot bones of an early amphibian (3). But the fin bones of lobefin (1) look so like the amphibian bones that this fish was probably the original fishy ancestor of land animals. Its name is *Eusthenopteron*.

Eusthenopteron is shown below emerging from the water, supporting itself on dry land on its fleshy, strong-boned fins. At a much later date, its amphibian descendants lived in swampy or marshy areas, returning to the water frequently, like frogs do today, to keep their skins moist. The amphibian shown here is *Ichthyostega*. It is the most ancient of all known amphibians, and so is probably the very first of all four-footed land animals.

What Makes a Land Animal?

If we compare a water animal such as a fish with a typical land animal, then we notice a number of strong differences.

The body of a fish is supported, or buoyed up, by the water, whereas the body of a land animal has to withstand the pull of gravity and so needs stouter and stronger bones.

A fish uses its gills to breathe the oxygen dissolved in the water in which it lives. But gills are no good for breathing air out of water. A few kinds of fishes have a lung-like organ as well as gills. It is from such organs that the air-breathing lungs of land animals have developed.

The skin of a fish will always stay moist as long as the fish is in water. The skin of a land animal, however, needs to withstand the drying action of sun and wind. The skin of amphibians—including the first land animals shown on this page—is still very like that of a fish, and this is one reason why amphibians are not *fully* land animals and need to return to the water occasionally.

Another reason amphibians must return to the water is to breed. The first *true* land animals, the reptiles, solved the problem of how to breed and reproduce on dry land. How they did this is told on the next page.

Amphibians and Reptiles

The first amphibians roamed the world 350 million years ago, but never strayed far from the water in which they hatched. Many lived in or near the shallow waters of the great coal swamps which covered large parts of the Earth's surface.

A large number of amphibians went back to living all their lives in water. These water-dwelling amphibians often stayed rather fish-like in appearance. And the young amphibians had gills, just as tadpoles of today have gills. The short legs and long, fish-like body of *Eogyrinus* (below) show that it would rarely have come out onto land. Yet *Eogyrinus* was one of a large group of amphibians whose descendants included the reptiles, the first true land animals, which lived 280 million years ago.

Not all early amphibians were reptile ancestors. Some, like *Diplocaulus*, were the ancestors of modern amphibians such as frogs and salamanders. The peculiar triangular head of *Diplocaulus* probably protected it against being swallowed by larger amphibians—or even by reptiles, which had begun to appear at the time it lived.

The reptiles were the first backboned creatures to spend all their time out of water.

Dimetrodon was a large early flesh-eating reptile.

Eogyrinus was an amphibian water-dweller with a long, rather fish-like body and small legs with webbed feet.

The first reptiles of all, such as *Hylonomus*, did not look very different from the smaller land-dwelling amphibians. Probably, if we could see *Hylonomus* alive, we would see that it was a reptile, and not an amphibian, from its drier skin. However, its skin did not survive as a fossil, only some of its bones. Geologists know that *Hylonomus* was a reptile from the particular number and shape of the bones of its skull.

How were they able to adjust to life on land? The chief secret of the first reptiles was their egg. An amphibian's egg is small and soft, like frogspawn, and will soon dry out and die if removed from the water. The much larger reptile egg is protected from drying out by its tough, waterproof shell. Safe inside its shell, the young reptile is nourished by a large supply of yolk until it is ready to hatch out.

Dimetrodon, the sailback reptile shown on the left, was one of the largest and most ferocious of the early reptiles. Its sail was really a heating-or-cooling fin. Turned towards the sunlight, it kept *Dimetrodon* warm. In the shade, the fin lost heat quickly, to cool *Dimetrodon* down.

Diplocaulus was an amphibian that lived about the same time as the large sailback reptile *Dimetrodon*, also shown above. Probably the two animals never met, because *Diplocaulus* spent most of its life on the beds of ponds or lakes, grubbing in the mud for its small prey.

11

Early Dinosaurs

Plateosaurus

Ornithosuchus

Millions of years ago	Geological name
	The
65	Tertiary Period
	Cretaceous Period
136	
	Jurassic Period
193	
	Triassic Period
225	
	Permian Period
280	
	Carboni- iferous Period

of the Dinosaurs

Age of Reptiles

Climate and plant life	Reptiles and other large animals
Much cooler. Many flowering plants.	End of the Age of Reptiles, beginning of the Age of Mammals.
Warm. The first flowering plants appeared.	The greatest meat-eating dinosaurs, such as *Tyrannosaurus*, preyed on other dinosaurs, such as *Triceratops*.
Becoming more humid. Even polar regions were warm and wet.	Dinosaurs became the dominant reptiles. They included the huge plant-eaters such as *Brachiosaurus*.
Very dry. Many deserts.	Many kinds of reptiles, including the first dinosaurs. Large sea reptiles such as plesiosaurs and ichthyosaurs.
Very warm and dry. The first conifers became common.	Ancestors of tortoises and turtles were common, as were primitive mammal-like reptiles and sailbacks.
Hot and swampy over many northern parts of the world.	End of the Age of Amphibians, beginning of the Age of Reptiles.

As the reptiles increased and flourished, they came to dominate the Earth. The amphibians, on the other hand, retreated and dwindled until they became the rather small and easily overlooked group of today.

The Age of Reptiles was a very long stretch of time—more than 200 million years—during which nearly every large animal that walked on land, swam in the water or glided in the air was a reptile.

The first large reptiles, including the sailbacks, gave way to a varied host of later types, including those most impressive of all reptiles, the dinosaurs. But a few very early types, such as the tortoises and turtles, plodded and shuffled on through the ages and are still living today.

We usually think of dinosaurs as nuge and ferocious creatures, but many were small. The earliest flesh-eating dinosaurs were rarely more than a few metres long, although they included ferocious fast runners such as *Ornithosuchus*, shown at full speed in the photo.

In the larger picture the same carnivorous dinosaur is attacking a larger but more harmless dinosaur, *Plateosaurus*. This was a herbivore or plant-eater, and grew up to 6 metres (20 feet) long.

The anatomy, or bone structure, of dinosaurs shows that they belong to two different groups. From the shape of their pelvis, or hip bone, these groups are called bird-hipped dinosaurs and reptile-hipped dinosaurs. Both the early dinosaurs shown here were reptile-hipped. Later reptile-hips included the greatest flesh-eaters such as *Tyrannosaurus* (page 18) and the greatest plant-eaters such as *Brachiosaurus* (pages 15 and 16). Bird-hipped dinosaurs—which were nothing like birds—included the large *Stegosaurus* (page 15) and horned dinosaurs (page 21).

Jurassic Giants

Camptosaurus

Brachiosaurus

Ornitholestes

The Jurassic age lasted for 58 million years. This is more than ten times as long as human beings have inhabited the Earth but it was only the first of the two dinosaur ages. The Jurassic dinosaurs included the largest of all land animals, the sauropods. They were herbivores, or plant-eaters, big enough to browse off the topmost leaves and branches of the tall prehistoric trees.

Brachiosaurus was a sauropod and the largest land animal ever, the heaviest creature to have walked the face of the Earth. More giant sauropods are shown overleaf.

Camptosaurus and *Stegosaurus* were other kinds of herbivorous dinosaurs of the Jurassic age. *Camptosaurus* probably walked on all fours but reared up on its hind legs when running or when brows-

Allosaurus

Stegosaurus

ing on the leaves of trees. *Stegosaurus* grew up to 7 metres (23 feet) long. These slow-moving giants always walked on all fours and fed by grazing the thick carpet of small ground plants. *Stegosaurus* must have been clumsy and stupid, but it was not an easy prey. It was protected by an armour of large bony plates along its back, and a sturdy tail armed with long, sharp spikes.

Smaller dinosaurs like *Ornitholestes* had no armour but had to rely on speed to flee from giant carnivorous dinosaurs in search of flesh to eat. The greatest flesh-eater of the time, *Allosaurus*, was a fearsome beast over 9 metres (30 feet) long with sharp teeth and long claws. Yet more terrifying carnivores were to succeed it in the Cretaceous, or second dinosaur age.

Peaceful Plant-eaters

Barosaurus
at 20 metres (66 feet), as long as three motor coaches

Sauropod Sizes and Weights

● Heaviest of sauropods was *Brachiosaurus*, with a maximum weight of 51 tonnes. It grew to 24 metres (79 feet) in length and could rear its head to a height of 12 metres (40 feet)—that is, as high as a three-storey house.
● *Apatosaurus*, also known as *Brontosaurus*, was another very heavily built sauropod, reaching a maximum length of about 20 metres (66 feet). You can see this giant compared with other giant animals on pages 34—35.
● *Diplodocus* was the longest of sauropods at 27 metres (89 feet) maximum. It was, however, more slimly built than *Brachiosaurus*, *Apatosaurus* and *Barosaurus*.

When fossils of giant sauropods were first reconstructed in the late 19th century, scientists were puzzled. How could such tiny heads with weak jaws eat enough to nourish such enormous bodies? They supposed that sauropods ate almost constantly throughout their lives, cramming themselves with bulky plant food.

Another puzzle was their great weight. A fully grown African elephant, largest of all land beasts today, weighs up to 8 tonnes and has thick, column-like legs to support this weight. But a giant sauropod could weigh more than six times as much, over 50 tonnes. How, then, could its legs, however thick, carry this huge load?

The 19th-century scientists answered this puzzle by supposing that the giant sauropods were amphibious beasts, who lived all their lives partly submerged in water which would help support their great weight. They would then have fed off vegetation growing in and around their native pools.

This was a neat solution, and one which was generally accepted until quite recently. But nature has many puzzles, and the answer turned out not to be the right one after all. Sauropods, it now seems, despite their size, were true land animals. A major piece of evidence is the shape of their feet, which are more like those of land-dwelling elephants than those of the water-dwelling hippopotamus. The ponderous sauropods filled a place in nature which is closest to that of those slimmer treetop browsers of today, the giraffes of Africa.

▲ The sauropods were so heavy that they could only just support their weight on four massive legs. Yet their skeletons, with longer hind legs and shorter forelegs, show that they descended from bipeds—creatures which, like us, walk erect on two legs.

◀ One of the largest sauropods, *Barosaurus*, lumbers away from a clump of trees where another *Barosaurus* is feeding.

▶ *Diplodocus*, the longest-ever land animal, had a surprisingly tiny head and puny teeth.

Dinosaurs

Terrible Teeth

The largest carnivorous reptiles to live before the dinosaurs were about 4 or 5 metres long (about 15 feet). That is, they were a bit bigger than today's lions and tigers. However, most flesh-eaters of the Permian and Triassic ages were smaller than this. The dinosaur carnivores that followed in the Jurassic and Cretaceous ages also varied greatly in size, but included many much greater and more alarming creatures.

● *Allosaurus* of the Jurassic age was more than 9 metres (30 feet) long and weighed much more than an elephant.

● *Gorgosaurus* and *Tarbosaurus* of the Cretaceous age were still larger.

● *Tyrannosaurus* of the late Cretaceous Period was largest of all, being 16 metres (52 feet) long, standing 6 metres (20 feet) high with a huge, dagger-fanged head 1·5 metres (5 feet) long.

The first age of dinosaurs, the Jurassic Period, ended 136 million years ago. The biggest of all dinosaurs, the giant, long-necked plant-eaters, had all died out, possibly because changes in climate had made the juicy plants they ate in such vast quantities less available.

The second age of dinosaurs, or Cretaceous Period, lasted even longer than the

The most fearsome of all dinosaurs, *Tyrannosaurus*, standing as high as a house, tears out the throat of a luckless duckbill dinosaur called *Corythosaurus*.

Rule

first age of dinosaurs—no less than 71 million years. It produced not only the most terrifying of all dinosaurs, *Tyrannosaurus*, but also a great variety of heavily protected plant-eaters with tough and knobbly skins which protected them like armour.

As the flesh-eaters grew ever larger and more terrible, so their vegetarian prey developed thicker, more impregnable armour-plating and longer and sharper spikes and horns. In a battle between a giant carnosaur and an armoured herbivore, perhaps the carnosaur usually won, but not without deep scars to show for it.

Early Carnosaurs

Flesh-eating dinosaurs, or carnosaurs, grew eventually to be the huge monsters shown below. But at first they were much smaller animals. Some early carnosaurs, such as the two shown above, were no larger than chickens. The one in front, holding a small lizard-like reptile in its jaws, is very unusual: its front legs have developed as flippers. It was probably an amphibious creature that spent part of its life in water, where its flippers would have been used for swimming.

Euoplocephalus was an armoured plant-eating dinosaur that well deserved the name of 'living tank'. But it was not entirely safe, because the teeth of giant carnosaurs, such as **Gorgosaurus** shown here, could penetrate even that thick armour of plates and spikes.

Armoured Dinosaurs

In the first, Jurassic, age of dinosaurs, some of the bigger plant-eaters, such as *Stegosaurus* (see page 15), were heavily armoured beasts which could defend themselves with vicious swishes of their long-spiked tails.

In the second, Cretaceous, age of dinosaurs, *Stegosaurus* was no longer around, but its place had been taken by a large variety of armoured plant-eaters having equally impregnable armour and impressive defensive weapons. They were in general much nimbler animals than the very slow and stupid *Stegosaurus*. They certainly needed all their strong armour and their extra speed, because the Cretaceous carnosaurs were even more terrible than the Jurassic ones.

One such Cretaceous armoured dinosaur was *Triceratops*, shown on the right. Although larger and heavier than an elephant of today, *Triceratops* was quick enough at getting away from its enemies. Not that it had many enemies, other than the very biggest carnosaurs, because it was more than able to

► *Triceratops*, seen here at a fast trot, weighed more than 8 tonnes yet was fairly nimble. Looking rather like an oversized rhino, but even more dauntingly armoured, it would have been opposed by very few other dinosaurs of its time.

► *Protoceratops*, seen here hatching from its eggs, was a fairly small, plant-eating dinosaur of the early Cretaceous age. Like the later, larger *Triceratops*, it had a large bony neck-shield which would have blunted the teeth of most aggressors.

◄ The heads of two bone-headed dinosaurs collide violently after a double charge. This strange behaviour was possibly a form of rivalry between males. Their long name *Pachycephalosaurus* is Latin for thick-headed reptile.

◄ *Triceratops'* skeleton, although huge and cumbrous when compared to a man, was more compact than those of most other dinosaurs. Its limbs did not sprawl awkwardly sideways like those of early reptiles, but were tucked neatly under the body—a sure sign of agility.

defend itself with its three long, sharp horns. Only the longest and sharpest teeth could have penetrated its thick hide, and even the teeth of the largest flesh-eaters would have skidded off its great bony neck-shield.

Other heavily armoured dinosaurs of the Cretaceous Period include the ankylosaurs, ('living tanks' shown on the previous page) and boneheads, called after their high, domed skulls which have survived well as fossils in the rocks, for example in Mongolia. These domed skulls consisted largely of a solid mass of bone, sometimes as much as 25 centimetres (10 inches) thick, surrounding the dinosaur's small brain. Why then did a bonehead have such a large thick skull? The answer seems to be that it employed its skull as a battering ram, when charging at an enemy or rival. However, so many of the skulls of these boneheads have survived intact as fossils, that we must suppose that such collisions did these dinosaurs no great harm.

The End of an Era

Dinosaurs died out about 65 million years ago, at the end of the Cretaceous Period. No fossils have been found in the rocks formed since then. No one has discovered exactly why dinosaurs became extinct so suddenly. Perhaps severe changes in the world's weather changed the kinds of plants that grew, leaving the plant-eating dinosaurs without their special food. As plant-eaters became more and more scarce, so too flesh-eating dinosaurs would have died out.

The world that came after the dinosaurs was more like our own. It was dominated by mammals and birds, animals that are most familiar today. Mammals had already been around for a very long time—all through the two dinosaur ages—but now, with the dino-

saurs gone, they increased in size and variety and soon became the dominant land animals. Plants, too, became more like those of today. The magnolia bush shown below is an early type of flowering plant that is seen in many gardens today.

Not all the dinosaurs' close relatives died out. The crocodile is a living cousin of the dinosaurs. But in number and variety the most successful descendants of the dinosaurs are the birds.

A scene in late Cretaceous times, not long before dinosaurs became extinct. Many of the other kinds of animals shown would outlive them.

Ornithomimus was a dinosaur that looked very like an ostrich. Like that bird it could easily outrun most of its enemies. It had plenty of these because its favourite food was the eggs of other dinosaurs.

Pterosaurs were winged reptiles related to the dinosaurs. They were gliders rather than real flyers (page 26). This one has glided much too close to the ground, and very likely will not be able to soar up into the air again.

The dinosaur with the bony head crest is called *Lambeosaurus*. It was a plant-eater belonging to a group known as the duckbilled dinosaurs.

Three other reptiles appear in this Cretaceous scene, and they are all types still living today. Immediately on the left are a pair of small lizards. On the far left, disappearing off the picture, is a legless lizard. Hauling itself out of the water onto the stream bank is a crocodile—the nearest living thing to a dinosaur.

The small mammal on the far left of the picture is an insectivore or insect-eater. After the long Cretaceous age, many other, larger mammals appeared, to replace the reptiles as the dominant land animals.

Swimming Reptiles

Throughout the Age of Dinosaurs, which lasted for 160 million years, the dinosaurs were the dominant land animals, but they were not the only reptiles to flourish during this vast stretch of time.

The oceans swarmed with relatives of the dinosaurs. The sea-serpent-like plesiosaurs and fish-like ichthysaurs shown here were among the reptiles that lived in the sea. Other large reptiles had already returned to the seas, lakes and rivers in an earlier age. Mosasaurs, like giant sea lizards, chased fishes and smaller reptiles through Triassic oceans.

Lurking in rivers and coastal waters were early crocodiles and the very similar phytosaurs, ready to snap at and drag into the water any unwary animals that came within range of their long, multi-toothed jaws.

Tortoises and turtles were more distant relatives of the dinosaurs. They appeared well before the Age of Dinosaurs, lived all through it, and continued to survive long after the dinosaurs and their closer relatives had vanished for ever.

On land, the warm-blooded and hairy mammals abounded throughout the Age of Reptiles, although they were small and insignificant, devouring insects and worms and living in the undergrowth. The air of Jurassic and Cretaceous times was filled with the leathery wings and bodies of pterosaurs, or gliding reptiles.

Peloneustes was a small, short-necked plesiosaur —a many-toothed fish-eater.

Reptiles That

Plesiosaurs were sea reptiles which at their largest—about 12 metres (40 feet) long—were the nearest living things to the mythical sea serpents, as they reared their long necks and humped backs out of the water. Other pleiosaurs, like that here, had shorter necks and larger heads. All plesiosaurs had four paddle-like limbs, with which they could have hauled themselves onto land to lay their eggs.

Relatives

▶ *Protosuchus* was an early type of crocodile which appeared during the Triassic Age. Its legs show that it was far less sluggish than its modern relatives.

▼ *Rutiodon* was a phytosaur. Although they were as large and as fierce as the later crocodiles, phytosaurs did not survive beyond Triassic times.

Returned to the Sea

Ichthyosaurs, whose name means fish-reptiles, were certainly the most fish-like of all dinosaur relatives. They were up to 3 metres (10 feet) long and looked like the porpoises of today. Like these sea mammals, they had to come to the surface every now and then to breathe air. Nevertheless, they were quite helpless on land and spent all their lives in the water. They gave birth to live young in the water.

Many ichthyosaur fossils have been found in the chalky coastal cliffs near Charmouth in Dorset, England.

▼ *Pteranodon*, seen here feeding its young, was a later pterosaur with the tremendous wingspan of 7 metres (23 feet)—much greater than that of any bird, living or extinct. Some gliding pterosaurs were even bigger. *Pteranodon* was toothless. It caught and carried fishes in large pouched jaws like those of a pelican.

Looking something like a character out of a Dracula film, *Dimorphodon* was a small, early pterosaur with a wingspan of less than a metre. It might have been able to flap its wings to keep itself airborne, but its large, heavy head, with great jaws filled with sharp teeth, would have weighed it down and made it a very clumsy flier indeed.

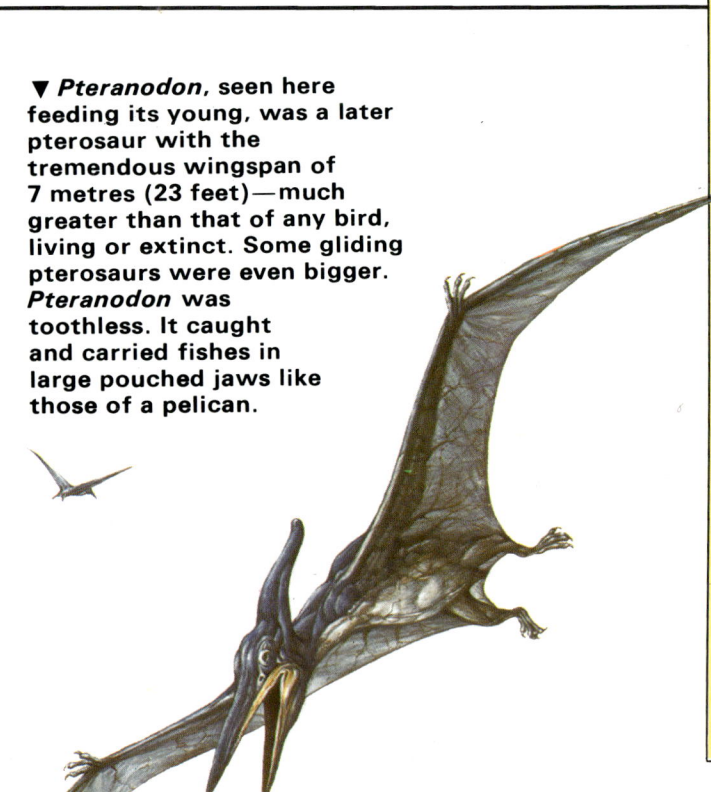

► Another small, early pterosaur from the Jurassic age, *Rhamphorynchus* had long jaws filled with many sharp, forward-pointing teeth. Almost certainly this shows that *Rhamphorynchus* was a fish-eater.

► *Archaeopteryx* is one of the two earliest birds. It had feathers and could fly, but was still very reptilian in many ways. Most obviously, its beak was filled with sharp reptilian teeth, and its wings bore four long claws.

Flying Reptiles

A small, fluffy bird is about the last animal we would associate with a vast, scaly dinosaur. Yet birds appeared on Earth at about the same time as the dinosaurs, and are quite closely related to them.

Only a very few fossils of these earliest birds have been found. *Archaeopteryx* and *Archaeornis*, as these fossil birds are called, were creatures of Jurassic times. They had long, running legs, a long, bony tail and a many-toothed beak. In these features they were very similar to many of the smaller dinosaurs who sped about on two legs at that time.

Two features of the fossil skeletons, however, distinguished them from all other reptiles. One is the long bones of the forelegs, including the greatly extended finger bones. These are the wing bones. The other is the clear imprint of feathers.

But unlike the skeletons of modern birds, those of the ancient fossils have a much smaller breastbone or sternum. This is the bone to which a bird's powerful flying muscles are attached. So the first birds, it appears, were weak flyers, perhaps spending most of their lives flapping heavily from tree to tree to get at fruits or other tree food.

The other reptiles of the air at this time were probably gliders, not flyers. They were the pterosaurs, whose leathery, somewhat bat-like wings were more weakly muscled even than those of the early birds. Some of the smaller pterosaurs could, perhaps, have flapped their wings from time to time, but most were gliders.

How a Fossil is Formed

Fossils are our main evidence for life in the distant past. We rely on fossils to tell us about dinosaurs and any other animal or plant which died more than a few thousand years ago. By this time the bodies of most dead creatures have long decayed, broken down by bacteria. Only a few creatures are preserved as fossils. But what exactly is a fossil?

The word fossil means 'something dug up' and we generally think of fossils as the remains of animals and plants which have become preserved in the rocks. This is, in fact, where most fossils are found, but some fossil insects have been preserved whole in the yellow, hard, transparent substance called amber, a sticky tree resin which turns solid over the years.

These fossil eggs provide evidence that dinosaurs were true, egg-laying reptiles.

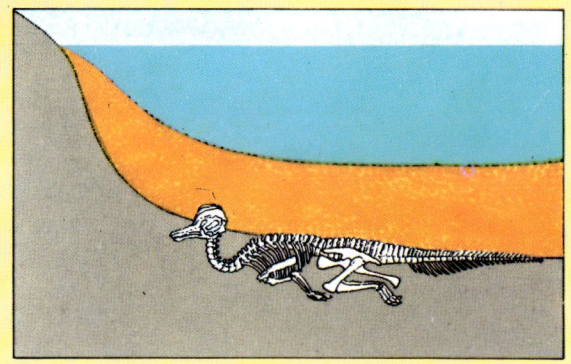

In the mud at the bottom of an ancient lake lies the skeleton of a plant-eating dinosaur called *Iguanodon*. All the softer parts of its body have decayed away.

A powdery layer of silt eventually covers the skeleton. Over the ages, under the weight of the upper layers, the lower layers of silt and mud change into rock.

The bony substance of the skeleton itself also becomes replaced by hard, rocky materials. After tens of millions of years, the rock wears away to reveal the fossil.

Relics

Animals and plants are also found preserved as fossils in tar lakes and peat bogs, places in which decay bacteria find it difficult to grow. Yet other fossils are found in ice, which is too cold to allow bacteria to grow. Complete fossil mammoths, hairy, extinct relatives of the elephant, have been discovered in the permanently frozen ground of Siberia.

Dinosaurs, however, were too large to have become fossilized in amber, and much too ancient to have been preserved whole in ice, which, because of changes in climate, would have melted long ago.

Dinosaurs left their bones in the rocks, as shown in the diagram on the left. Only their bones and other hard parts were preserved in this way. All their soft parts decayed away or were removed by the crushing action of heavy rock, before they had time to fossilize.

Teeth make good fossils because they are hard and do not quickly disappear by decay. This large biting tooth, 17 cm (6·7 inches) long, is a fossil from the Jurassic age, and so may have once belonged to the great flesh-eater *Allosaurus*.

◄ Not only the bones, teeth, claws and eggs of dinosaurs became fossilized. These footprints were made long ago in soft ground, which later hardened into rock. The dinosaur which left the fossil footprints is called *Megalosaurus* and lived in the Jurassic age.

Dinosaur Hunters

Othniel March and Edward Cope, framed below, were rival American dinosaur hunters of the last century. They discovered many fossils in the Midwest.

▲ A scientist in Mongolia uncovers the fossil bones of the large flesh-eating dinosaur *Tarbosaurus*.

Othniel Marsh 1831–1899

Hunting for fossils first became popular in the early 19th century. Fossil hunters of Europe and America included both professional scientists and ordinary people interested in the history of life, or merely in collecting fossils.

Many rocks and cliffs contain innumerable fossils of sea shells and the hard parts of other small creatures. In softer rocks, such as clay and limestone, these are easy enough to dig out of the rock with a penknife, or better, a geological hammer.

Much larger fossils, such as those of dinosaurs and their relatives, can only be uncovered fully, or removed entirely from the surrounding rock, by special techniques. Many of these techniques were invented by 19th-century dinosaur hunters, including the two portrayed on these pages.

Fossils started scientists arguing about how animals and plants have changed through the ages. These arguments eventually became the theory of evolution.

▼ The Gobi desert of Outer Mongolia is cold and hostile, but it is a rich source of dinosaur fossils. Several expeditions have been sent to the Gobi. This one was in 1925.

So many dinosaur fossils have been discovered in the Midwest of the USA that they are often not removed to museums. Instead they are cleaned and left displayed in their native rock.

Edward Cope 1840–1897

A fossil hunter in Africa brushes away dirt and loose rock from the fossil skull of a reptile, possibly a small dinosaur.

▲ He covers the loosened fossil first in tissue paper, then in sacking soaked in wet plaster. This hardens as it dries into a protective covering.
Above right: Each of the fossils are then separately labelled, before they are packed away in stout wooden cases for their long journey to the museum.

Rebuilding a Dinosaur

You have probably seen skeletons of dinosaurs and other fossil animals on display in museums. The fossil bones of any complete skeleton will have been assembled and wired together by experts into an accurate lifelike position.

However, it is quite rare for fossil bones to be so tidily arranged in nature. Even the bones of a partial fossil, such as those of a skull, may be broken up in the rocks into small pieces. They have to be put together in the right order before a particular fossil animal becomes recognizable. Larger bones may also be scattered and jumbled together in their native rocks, as shown in the photo on page 31.

Removing a fossil skeleton from its native rock is always a delicate process, and may take years rather than days. The fossil hunter carefully chips away at the rock surrounding

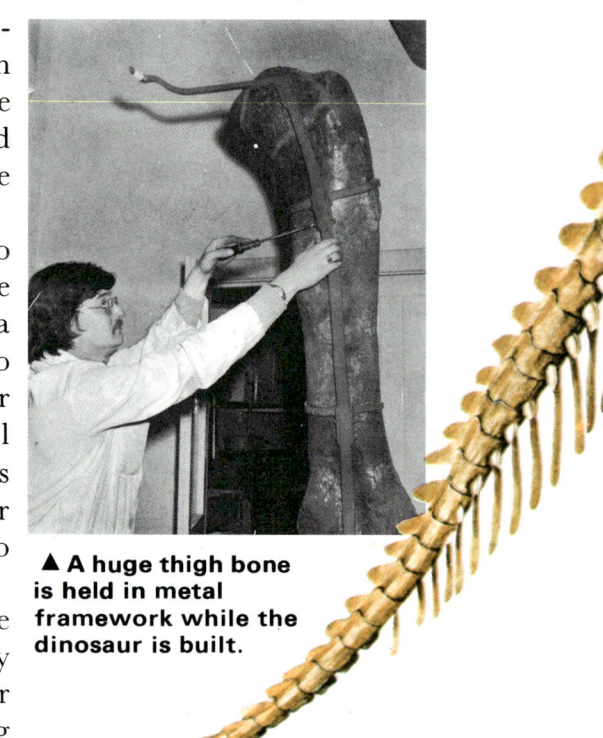

▲ A huge thigh bone is held in metal framework while the dinosaur is built.

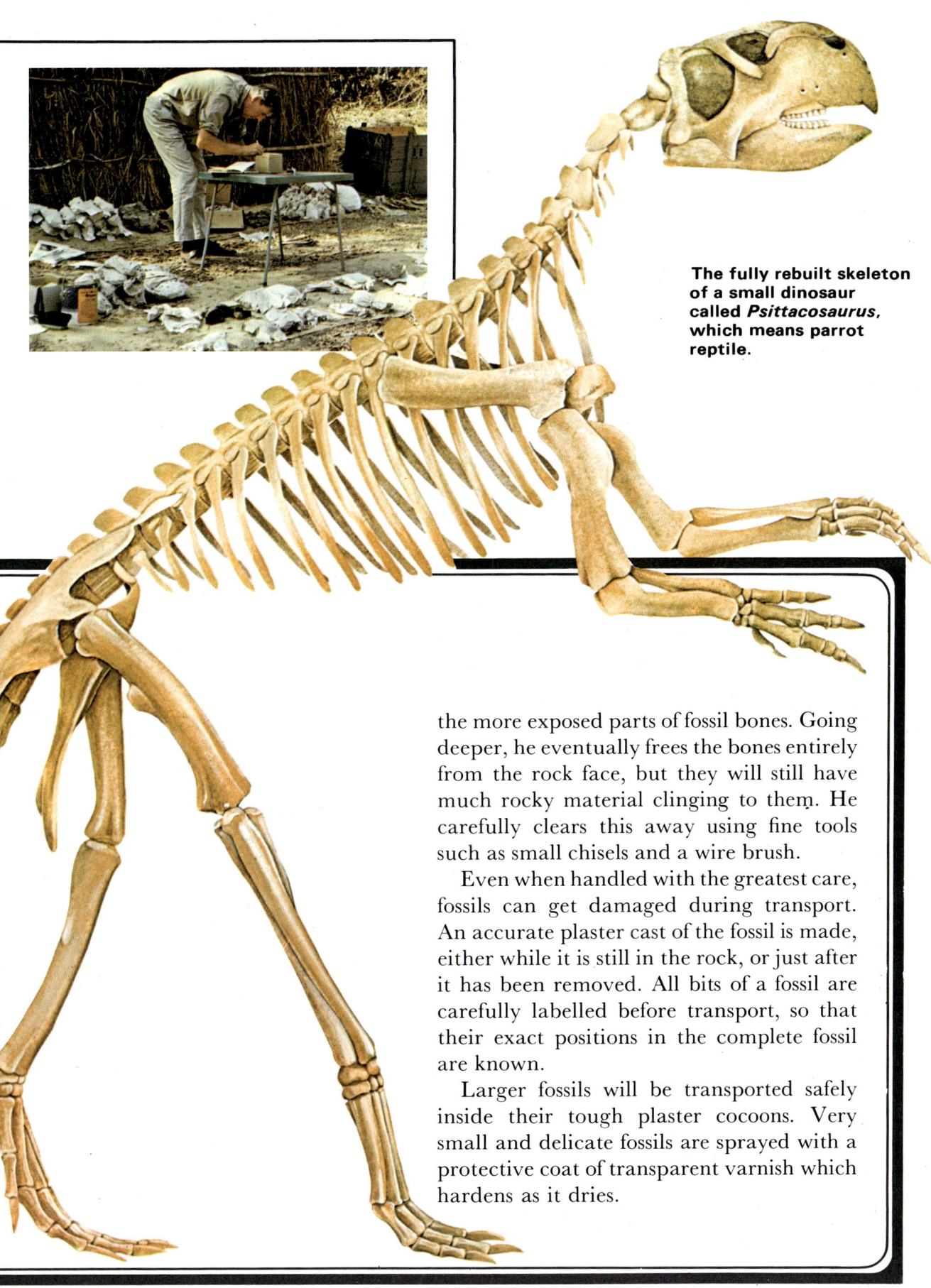

The fully rebuilt skeleton of a small dinosaur called *Psittacosaurus*, which means parrot reptile.

the more exposed parts of fossil bones. Going deeper, he eventually frees the bones entirely from the rock face, but they will still have much rocky material clinging to them. He carefully clears this away using fine tools such as small chisels and a wire brush.

Even when handled with the greatest care, fossils can get damaged during transport. An accurate plaster cast of the fossil is made, either while it is still in the rock, or just after it has been removed. All bits of a fossil are carefully labelled before transport, so that their exact positions in the complete fossil are known.

Larger fossils will be transported safely inside their tough plaster cocoons. Very small and delicate fossils are sprayed with a protective coat of transparent varnish which hardens as it dries.

Dinosaurs

Size and Shape

Dinichthys was a giant fish, a placoderm, which became extinct nearly 400 million years ago. It was 9 metres (30 feet) long, and heavy-bodied.

Meganeura lived about 320 million years ago. These giant dragonflies with wingspans up to 80 cm (31 inches) were the largest insects ever.

Apatosaurus, or *Brontosaurus* as this dinosaur was first called, was one of the largest land animals ever to have lived. *Apatosaurus* was over 20 metres (66 feet) long and weighed about 45 tonnes. It lived about 180 million years ago.

Iguanodon was a medium-sized dinosaur. It stood 4·5 metres (15 feet) tall and was 8 metres (26 feet) long. It lived about 130 million years ago.

Protoceratops was a smallish dinosaur that lived about the same time as *Iguanodon*. It was about 3 metres (10 feet) long.

Pteranodon was a giant flying reptile with a wingspan of 7 metres (23 feet). It lived about 130 million years ago.

Archaeopteryx was a very early bird. It lived about 180 million years ago.

Baluchitherium was the largest land mammal ever. It stood about 8·5 metres (28 feet) high, and lived about 30 million years ago.

Diatryma was a giant bird, over 2 metres (6·5 feet) high, that lived about 45 million years ago.

Procoptodon was a giant kangaroo, 3 metres (10 feet) high. It lived in Australia about 2 million years ago.

Dinosaurs came in all sizes and included the biggest of all land animals. Here, three dinosaurs are compared in size with some of the largest among other kinds of extinct animals, and also with man.

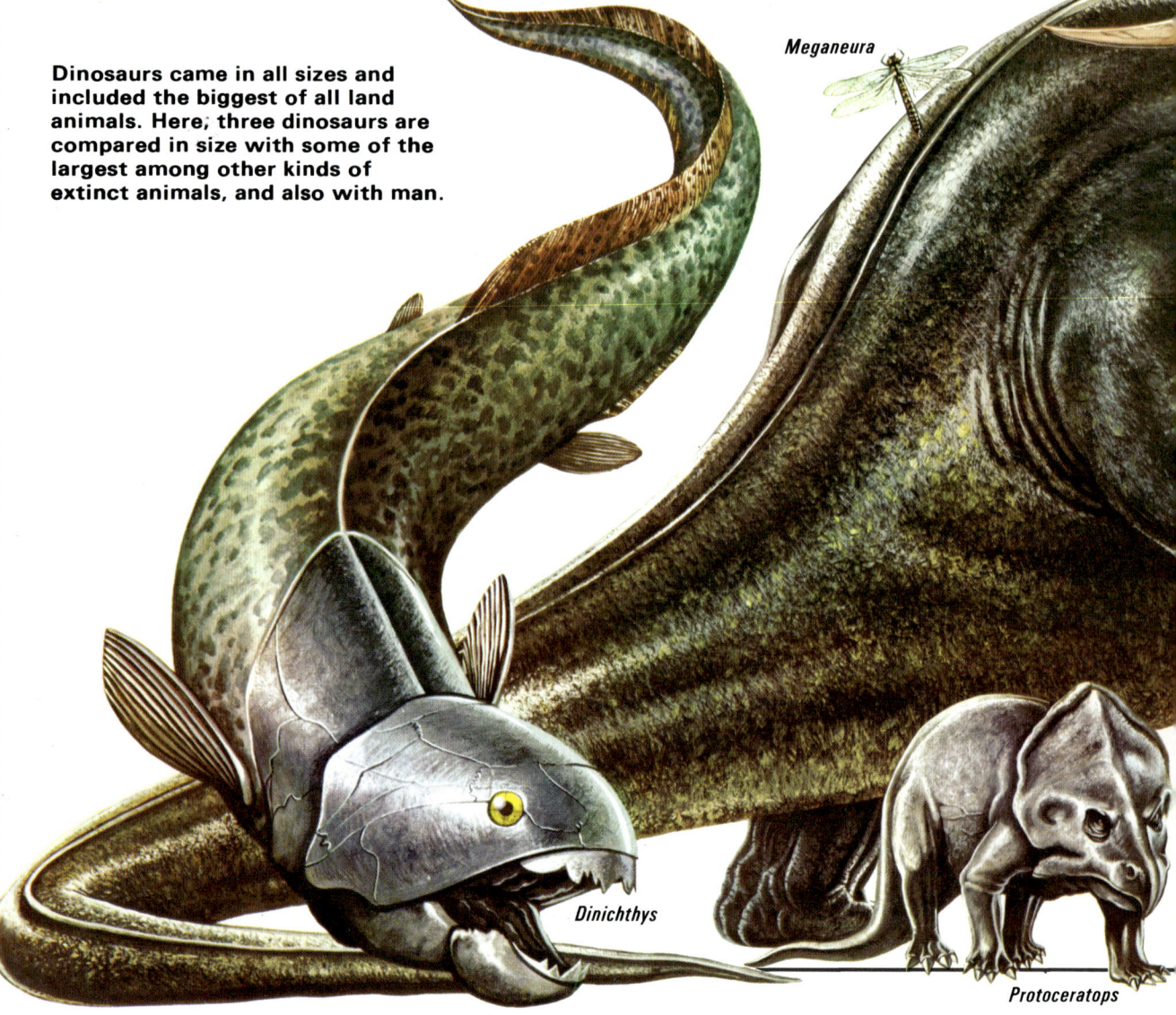

Meganeura

Dinichthys

Protoceratops

Compared

Pteranodon

Apatosaurus

Archaeopteryx

Baluchitherium

Iguanodon

Procoptodon

Diatryma

Dinosaur Family Tree

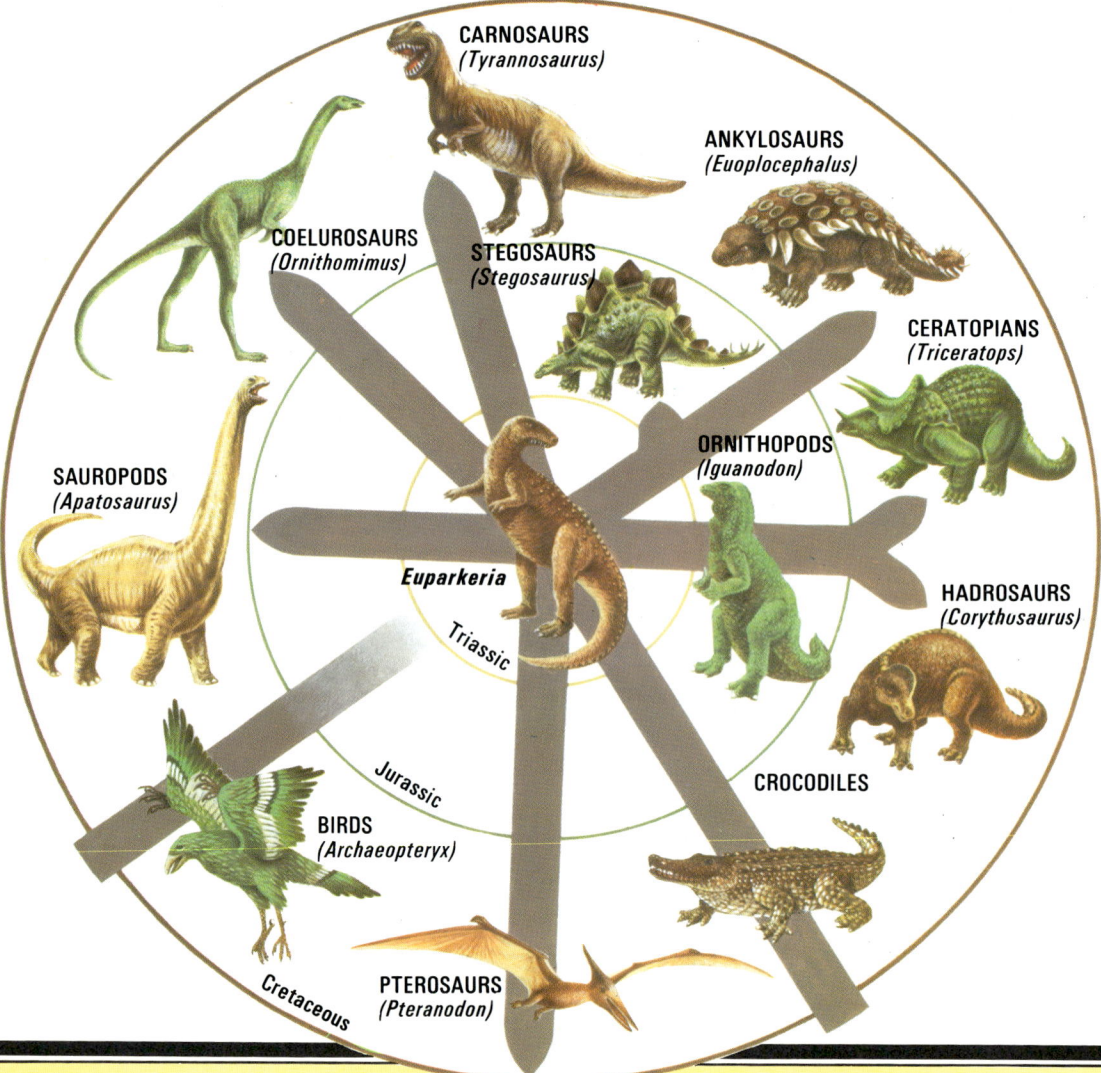

CARNOSAURS
(*Tyrannosaurus*)

ANKYLOSAURS
(*Euoplocephalus*)

COELUROSAURS
(*Ornithomimus*)

STEGOSAURS
(*Stegosaurus*)

CERATOPIANS
(*Triceratops*)

ORNITHOPODS
(*Iguanodon*)

SAUROPODS
(*Apatosaurus*)

Euparkeria

Triassic

HADROSAURS
(*Corythosaurus*)

Jurassic

CROCODILES

BIRDS
(*Archaeopteryx*)

Cretaceous

PTEROSAURS
(*Pteranodon*)

The family tree diagram shows dinosaurs and their close relatives. In the centre is a small dinosaur ancestor, the reptile *Euparkeria* which lived in the Triassic age. This was one of a group of reptiles called thecodonts, which gave rise to the various groups of dinosaurs. Sauropods, coelurosaurs, carnosaurs, stegosaurs, ankylosaurs, ornithopods, ceratopians, and hadrosaurs are all dinosaurs.

Euparkeria and its relatives were also the ancestors of many other later reptiles. These are the remaining groups shown in the diagram, namely, the crocodiles, pterosaurs and birds.

The tortoises, turtles, tuatara, mosasaurs, plesiosaurs and ichthyosaurs are reptiles not so closely related to the dinosaurs and so are not on the family tree. Of the animals on the tree, only the crocodiles and birds are still alive today.

Index

Acknowledgements

Cover Imitor; Endpapers Pat Morris; 20 Imitor; 26 NHPA; 28 Imitor; 29 Imitor *top*, Pat Morris *bottom*; 30 Zophia Kielan-Jawarowska *top*, American Museum of Natural History *centre, bottom left*; 31 Pat Morris *top*, American Museum of Natural History *bottom right*; 32 Barry Cox *top left* and *right*; Imitor *bottom*; 33 Barry Cox.

Picture research: Penny Warn and Jackie Cookson.